Calisthenics

The Ultimate Beginner's Calisthenics Bodyweight Exercises Guide & Workout Training Routines + 30-Day Greek God Muscle Building Action Plan Challenge

By *Jennifer Louissa*

For more great books visit:

HMWPublishing.com

Download another book for Free

I want to thank you for purchasing this book and offer you another book (just as long and valuable as this book), "Health & Fitness Mistakes You Don't Know You're Making", completely free.

Visit the link below to signup and receive it:

www.hmwpublishing.com/gift

In this book, I will break down the most common health & fitness mistakes, you are probably committing right now, and I will reveal how you can easily get in the best shape of your life!

In addition to this valuable gift, you will also have an opportunity to get our new books for free, enter giveaways, and receive other valuable emails from me. Again, visit the link to sign up:

www.hmwpublishing.com/gift

Table Of Contents

Introduction 8

    Have Injuries? 11

Chapter 2 - Avoid Theses Calisthenics Mistakes ... 13

    Here is a list of most common mistakes that beginners make: 13

        ➢ Lack of focus: 13

        ➢ Training with high reps only: 13

        ➢ No consistency: 14

        ➢ The absence of goals: 14

        ➢ Progressing too fast: 14

Chapter 3 - What Advantages Do I Gain From Calisthenics Compared To Other Workouts? 16

    Free Exercise At Home With No Equipment 16

    Full Body Workout 17

    Lose Fat Effectively 17

    Develop Endurance 18

Much safer than modern workout techniques.....19

Chapter 4 - Best Beginner Calisthenics Exercises 20

Pull-ups and Chin-ups 21

Pushups..22

Superman Push-Ups 23

Squats..25

Burpees and Mountain Climbers....................27

Mountain Climbers 28

Prisoner Squats 29

Lunges..30

Dips 32

Sit-ups 33

Crunches..35

Dorsal Raises..36

Oblique V-Ups...37

The critical points for these workouts are............38

Tips for Beginners..39

Calisthenics Abs 41

Calisthenics Arms 44

Calisthenics Legs 45

The 10 Directives of Calisthenics Muscle Mass.... 47

- ➢ DIRECTIVE 1: Embrace reps! 47
- ➢ DIRECTIVE 2: Work Hard! 47
- ➢ DIRECTIVE 3: Use Simple, Compound Exercises! 47
- ➢ DIRECTIVE 4: Reduce Sets! 47
- ➢ DIRECTIVE 5: Concentrate on progress and use a Training dairy! 47
- ➢ DIRECTIVE 6: You rise if you Rest. So feel free to take rest! 47
- ➢ DIRECTIVE 7: keep eating clean the whole Time! 47
- ➢ DIRECTIVE 8: Sleep well! 47
- ➢ DIRECTIVE 9: Train your mind while training your Body! 47
- ➢ DIRECTIVE 10: Get Strong! 48

How Can You Do Those Exercises At Home Or In The Street?..48

The Lean & Mean Calisthenics Diet......................49

Here's the strategy for success with this diet:......50

- ➢ Eat As Natural As Possible 50
- ➢ Eat Produce, Organic when Possible...50
- ➢ Get Your Protein IN 51
- ➢ Grains and Dairy..................................52
- ➢ Keep a Food Diary: 54

Chapter 6 - Mistakes To Avoid In Your Diet .55

- ➢ Mistake 1: Eating unhealthy, processed food. 56
- ➢ Mistake 2: Not getting enough protein.56

Chapter 7 - 30-Day Calisthenics Challenge ...59

The Challenge...61

Squats..61

Reverse Lunge 62

Shoulder Press 62

Push Ups 63

Diamond Press Up 64

Reverse Crunch 64

Burpees 65

Final Words **67**

About The Co-Author **69**

Introduction

I want to thank you and congratulate you for downloading the *"Calisthenics for Beginners"* book. This book contains proven steps and strategies on how to perform calisthenics exercises at home or in the street and includes everything you need to get started in the right direction safely. You'll also discover what exactly calisthenics is all about and what are the crucial mistakes you must avoid when performing theses exercises. Moreover, you'll learn the advantages of Calisthenics compared to other workouts and will share with you some of the best beginner exercises to get the most impactful results. Likewise, will also explain and reveal the best methods to build muscle as well as share with you the most common diet mistakes that people make and how you can avoid this pitfall. Lastly, we also provide you with a 30-day exercise routine, which you can get started right away!

Also, before you get started, I recommend you **joining our email newsletter** to receive updates on any upcoming new book releases or promotions. You can sign-up for free, and as a bonus, you will receive a free gift. Our *"Health & Fitness*

Mistakes You Don't Know You're Making" book! This book has been written to demystify, expose the top do's and don'ts and to finally equip you with the information you need to get in the best shape of your life. Due to the overwhelming amount of mis-information and lies told by magazines and self-proclaimed "gurus", it's becoming harder and harder to get reliable information to get in shape. As opposed to having to go through dozens of biased, unreliable and un-trustworthy sources to get your health & fitness information. Everything you need to help you has been broken down in this book for you to easily follow and to immediately get results to achieve your desired fitness goals in the shortest amount of time.

Once again, to join our free email newsletter and to receive a free copy of this valuable book, please visit the link and signup now: **www.hmwpublishing.com/gift**

Chapter 1 – What Is Calisthenics?

Even if the name seems weird, you probably have already tried calisthenics without knowing! If you ever performed push-ups, crunches and other related stuff like that then you've probably been doing calisthenics. Calisthenics is exercises including a variety of bodily movements generally without using equipment or apparatus using little to no added weight, and it is commonly known as a body-weight workout. Calisthenics training can be released as a daily routine training, or following workout programs and plans. It's convenient and has many advantages, and it can be adapted to suit beginner, intermediate or advanced trainees.

Calisthenics is for everyone, one of its best things is that it provides plenty of training exercises for all levels. Calisthenics is a matter of progressing, and just because you find difficulties and you begin from a low level, doesn't mean that you won't have good results. So start at your level -the level that you feel comfortable- just make sure to keep going. The more you train, the sooner you'll find yourself progressing through the stages. Calisthenics is the solution for any working people leading busy lives, forced to travel away from home. The office space, a hotel room, public parks; just anywhere there is some open space to move around safely calisthenics is possible.

Have Injuries?

Calisthenics is also excellent for recovering from an injury. If you have been injured because of physical activity or in your daily life, starting calisthenics will allow you to take a step back and re-evaluate that specific area. Some sports injuries caused by weakened tendons and muscles; swift and long-lasting recovery comes from strengthening that area. Calisthenics will let you take back your strength training and invigorate that zone.

Calisthenics advantages will not only benefit you now, but that will also support you in the future. It allows you to keep or stay flexible, high core endurance for abdominal muscles and lower back, have actively support joints and ensures you maintain good posture. Keeping yourself fit and healthy now will also allow you to be free of aches and pains in your elderly years; it's the secret of well being.

Chapter 2 - Avoid Theses Calisthenics Mistakes

Evidently, getting stronger with calisthenics isn't a straightforward thing. As a result, lots of us, especially beginners make mistakes while training.

Here is a list of most common mistakes that beginners make:

> **Lack of focus:**

Beginners make quite often this mistake when they don't feel any progress or they progress slower than expected. So they are changing training programs and goals too fast.

> **Training with high reps only:**

Certainly it isn't bad! High reps are essential for endurance. But it isn't going to make you stronger. In fact, you won't see much psychical change to your body. Many people will do a workout and not count the reps but go as many as they can. This is also not a bid deal, but you only won't see fast change. You need to keep your reps between 8 to 12 reps. It blocked my strength training progress when I was young when I used to the mistake of going as many reps as I could then saw my friend doing 8 reps with a slower and more controlled movement

➢ **No consistency:**

The lack of discipline and motivation involve a lack of consistency. The only way to get strong is to be consistent and make your workout a habit.

➢ **The absence of goals:**

Missing goals lead to the lack of focus decreases motivation and causes boredom. So setting goals is an essential element of successful training.

➢ **Progressing too fast:**

This is an error that I have fallen into; I didn't spend

the necessary time to prepare and to form the proper foundation. It's dangerous and may lead to an injury and stops your progress and I expect you don't want to get in such situation. You have to avoid this by sticking to the progressions and using some common sense.

Chapter 3 - What Advantages Do I Gain From Calisthenics Compared To Other Workouts?

Free Exercise At Home With No Equipment

The most noticeable benefit of calisthenics is that you almost do not need any equipment or a lot of space to work out. In other words, you don't have to leave home! This brings additional benefits: regarding time efficiency. This means you don't have to waste time to go to the gym, and then back home. Calisthenics does not need any gym equipment or machines and can be performed in your own home; thus, calisthenics is one of the most practical training exercises. And since you don't have to leave the house, you don't have to bother with traveling costs. Calisthenics is 100% free so don't waste your money paying for expensive gym memberships while you could be making better use of that cash. Overall, you can perform calisthenics exercises anywhere, anytime.

Full Body Workout

Calisthenics targets a variety of muscle groups within a single exercise. Most of the calisthenics exercises engage more than one muscle group. Even more, these muscles have to work with accordance and harmonize in the right moment. The example below shows that each exercise involves multiple muscle groups at the same time and when you add more workouts with little to no rest between it is called a "superset."

Lose Fat Effectively

If you're want to lose fat, calisthenics is one of the most efficient ways of accomplishing this. Your training should involve some strength exercises and include some cardio. Just doing your workout with little to no rest can be seen as a form of cardio since you're raising your heart rate in the "fat burning zone." It's necessary to lose weight more efficiently and build muscles as well as strengthening the soft tissue. Calisthenics can easily be performed with high intensity, and that's why it is efficient as a fat fighter.

Develop Endurance

Adequately performed calisthenics exercise in the adjusted number of reps and sets can undoubtedly increase your body endurance. Particularly for muscle endurance and body-weight exercises, which demand that you hold a still position an extended period. The visual example under is called "The Plank," it is one of many exercises that you can do holding a position for a duration. This can also be seen as a form of endurance stretching. It is incredible for lower back pain and to keep your core tight.

Much safer than modern workout techniques

Calisthenics movements are natural and smooth. Our body weight is the maximum weight we are moving, and it's something our muscles are used to doing.

Chapter 4 - Best Beginner Calisthenics Exercises

For every beginner, the most significant thing is undoubtedly building your base strength. And to develop a robust base, this is necessary to focus on essential exercises such as Pull-Ups, Push-Ups, Leg Raises, and Squats. These are the basics, and the basics are what works and help you progress the most. Those who look for fast results will probably try to progress quicker, but as they enhance and try to teach a new competency, they may find problems because they are poorly performing those basic exercises.

Calisthenics, as bodyweight exercises, are exercises that don't need the use of equipment to work your muscles and raise your heart rate. Calisthenic common exercise includes push-ups, chin-ups, pull-ups, dips, burpees, sit-ups, jumping jacks, crunches, running in place and mountain climbers. To make the exercise easier or more difficult you can, for example, change the placement of your hands while doing pull-ups or other exercises. Trainings that requires you to use your legs will not be easy if you have knee or lower back issues. Exercises that put more pressure on smaller muscles, such as the triceps, will also be harder than those that involve primarily larger muscles, such as the biceps.

Pull-ups and Chin-ups

The standard calisthenics for building upper-body strength is Pull-ups and chin ups. Pull-ups, because they rely more on triceps and Latissimi Dorsi a.k.a "lats" than biceps and pectorals, are more difficult than chin-ups. Perform them slowly pausing after reps and using muscular effort to bring down yourself in place of dropping down with gravity to make the exercise more difficult.

• **PULLUP (OVERHAND GRIP)**
Compared against the chinup, the pullup better activates your lower traps—key players in the quest for a V-shaped torso. It also works your lats and infraspinatus muscles, which help rotate your shoulder joints.

• **CHINUP (UNDERHAND GRIP)**
Although technically a back exercise, the chinup also activates your biceps and pectoral muscles. If you find pullups too hard, give chinups a try.

Pushups

Until building upper body strength, beginners can deal with pushups done from a kneeling stance. Doing the plank position, pushups are harder if you place your hands farthest and perform the reps heavily. A more advanced form of calisthenics push-ups is called the Superman push-up and incline pushups and are even more defiant.

Superman Push-Ups

Superman Push-ups are performed with arms straight instead of bent, needing you to use fewer biceps and more triceps. Incline pushups are performed at a 45-degree angle, with your head towards the ground and your feet on a bench, or your hands on a bench and your feet toward the ground.

The example below shows you the final position of the superman-push-up.

You start off in by doing a standard push up and as you go up instead of slowly going back up; use a full burst motion and try to push yourself off the ground to be air-born. This takes a lot of practice, and the most challenging part is getting your feet off the ground using the energy from your chest and arms and abs since it is your lower abs controlling your legs to stay straight-plank up like Superman flying. Great way to impress people too!

Squats

Squats are one of the essential exercises that you should include in your calisthenic workout to build lower body strength. Stand with your toes pointed forward and your feet shoulder-width aside. Start the movement by lowering the hips and bending the knees into a squat position keeping your torso between your legs. Round off the action by thrusting the hips forward and straightening the knees to get back to a standing position. Variations of squat techniques include wall squats and sumo squats for beginners and one-legged or overhead squats for those who are at a high-level training.

or with weight (you can also use Dumbbells by hanging them on each side as you go down instead of over your shoulder like this image here utilizing a barbell bar).

Burpees and Mountain Climbers

Because of the amount of effort they require, Burpees and mountain climbers are challenging to perform for long periods, but they are easy to learn. During a burpee, you have to move quickly from a standing position to a crouch, then kick back your legs to get a plank position. Before you return to the crouch position, you can perform a pushup using or without a handclap; then you stand back up. To make mountain climbers, get in a runner's crouch position with your hands in front of your shoulders and butt pointed upward, then kick your legs back as if you are running up a hill on all fours one at a time as the other comes forward.

Burpee exercise: If you cannot the step #7 (the jump due to knee or leg injury) just do a small hop but keep your core tight with your arms over your head.

Mountain Climbers

As if you are climbing a vertical mountain bending your knees and squeezing simultaneously.

Prisoner Squats

While stretching your chest and shoulders the prisoner squat targets all of the muscles in your lower body. Stand with your fingertips touching the back of your head and your feet shoulder-width apart. Lift your chest and push your elbows back and bend your knees, push your hips back, and squat until your thighs are parallel to the floor. Stand back up and then redo. Do not lean too far forward just keep your weight on your heels. Try to maintain your shoulders on your feet at all times.

Just like a person being caught in the act; put your hands behind your head and drop. When you watch prison movies or series and always wished you could have a body of the big prisoner well this is your chance! :)

Lunges

Lunges target leg flexibility, strength, and endurance. Like the squat position, start the lunge movement by straight position with the feet shoulder-width aside, and the toes pointed forward. Come on with one leg while bending at the hips and knees until you attain a lower position with both knees bent at a maximally 90-degree angle. With the same leg used to move forward, push up and return to the starting stance. Ranges of lunge techniques expand from basic, easy lunges for beginners to back and side lunges for the more advanced ones.

Dips

Dips are exercises to practice on a bench, using two chairs or bars. You raise and lower yourself with your legs straight or at an angle in front of you or behind you. You can perform chair dips at home so that you press with your hands on the backs of two chairs, fold your knees backward and cruise your ankles behind you, and you finish by raising and low yourself. If you are looking to make it harder, move your hands even with or slightly behind your hips to make your triceps and lats work more. Another variation demands performing dips against your couch, with your legs straight out and your hands behind you. Put your feet on the floor, then raise yourself up and down.

Sit-ups

Old-fashioned sit-ups are a perfect way to strengthen the abs and hip flexors. There is some deficiency of the functionality in this movement on the flat ground, as a flat surface does not enable most person's abs to engage when they start the movement correctly. Sit-ups can be done with the feet fixed or not. Having the fix feet raise the rate at which sit-ups can be affected, which intensifies the metabolic exigency but also shifts the recruitment more to the hip flexors.

Put the soles of your feet at the same time, with knees discard out to the sides, an AbMat or another support under your lower back, and roll slowly up into a fully upright sitting stance, with no jerking in the motion to take the hip flexors out of the movement and need the abs to do the work. To vary the charge on sit-ups, you can do them on an incline or decline, like the push-ups. You can also change your arm position to neaten the difficulty of the movement. Keeping both straight arms overhead, by the ears, is more difficult than maintaining the arms by the sides. Holding weight at the chest or overhead further increases the requirements.

Crunches

Crunches are harder than sit-ups because your shoulders never touch the ground, keeping your muscles in use all the time. Alterations like the bicycle kicks that move your body from side to side as you stamp your legs with back and forth movement, and side oblique crunches, improve the difficulty because you move your body without the use of the arms and legs.

Dorsal Raises

Throughout this exercise, keep your feet on the floor and your legs straight. Your forehead resting on the floor your hands placed behind your lower back and you lie on your front. Raise-up your head and chest 6 or so inches off the floor and then smoothly return to the starting stance. Only push up the maximum you feel comfortable. Let this exercise be more difficult by placing your hands on your temples.

Oblique V-Ups

A calisthenics workout routine would not be complete without an abdominal exercise such the oblique V-ups. Start the movement lying on one of your sides keeping your legs outstretched from the hips at a 30-degree angle. Keep your right arm on the floor and place your left hand behind your head. Keeping them straight, stir up your legs from the floor, lead the torso toward the leg, and then gently return to the starting stance. Complete repetitions as you want on both sides.

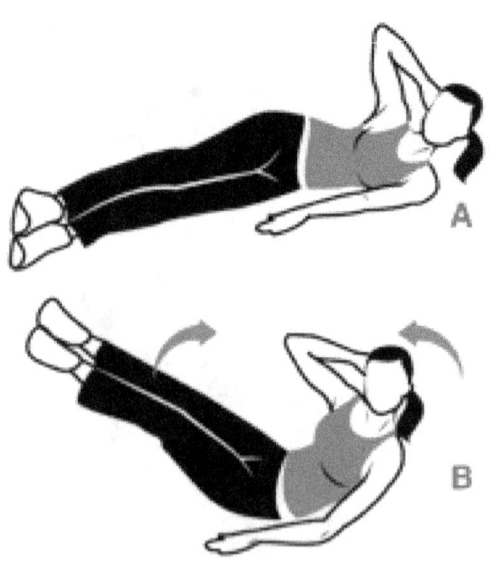

These are some of the basic Calisthenics workouts. Most of them are used to reinforce your hand strength and grip your core, scapula, straight-arm strength as well as training your nervous system.

The critical points for these workouts are

- Concentrate on quality more than quantity.
- Feel free to take more rest time between positions, exercises, and rounds.
- If a particular exercise seems difficult, find a more comfortable variation and build up from there.
- Remember to keep pushing yourself.
- Feel free to take more rest time between positions, exercises, and rounds.

Calisthenics workouts are fantastic for quick results since you're using many muscles at the same. It's kind of like you are doing a "superset" of movements. After a couple of weeks, of doing these basics workout, you can then move on to a more advance Calisthenics workouts such as Upper body mobility, core mobility, lower body mobility workouts as well as flexibility.

Tips for Beginners

It's important to start with the basics as with everything in life! Before you look at performing the human flag, muscle-ups, and front lever you need to build a strong base. Always do stretching exercises after and before your calisthenics exercises to avoid injuries and strains. Stretching certainly helps to get more flexibility and it is beneficial for muscle recuperation.

A common mistake of beginners is that they do not do the exercises correctly. I have seen a lot of people giving street workout up after a short period because they did not see any results. This was mostly due because they did not perform the exercises correctly. It is better doing 5 pushups accurately than do 10 improper ones. You cannot build strong muscles if you don't control the motion.

If you feel a part of your body is delicate, add more exercises to boost it. You have to discover calisthenics yourself to attain your goals.

Please keep in mind that any calisthenics exercise should be done with proper technique, form, and breathing. Incorrectly performing any callisthenic workout may cause unnecessary strain to your joints. When executed properly, any calisthenics exercise is fun and very efficient.

Chapter 5- Calisthenics Methods To Build Real Muscle

When thinking about it, it wasn't that long ago that the most muscular men in the world didn't have gym equipment or access to free weights to get muscle size and strength. Instead, they relied on calisthenics, and body weight training to get bigger, faster, and stronger. Thus, you are on the right track to begin a workout, which can help you to get bigger, and toned muscles without going to a gym.

Calisthenics Abs

The calisthenics body begins in the middle because you use your abs for every single exercise when you train with bodyweight. Where the standard form of working abs is using the machine at the gym; calisthenics abs are built using movements like leg raise, full-ROM hanging, and windshield wipers. Since they rely strongly on the serratus anterior in addition to the muscles you always think of when we talk about abdominals, these movements have a direct impact on the trunk's overall appearance. This has a significant effect in shaping and framing the entire abdominal region. The marking of the calisthenics body is a serratus with the steak-knife edge, and the bulging six-pack abs hold within. This is why when you Google search image: Calisthenics; you get people with nice abs or 6 packs.

Calisthenics Back, Shoulders and Chest

Wide lats are particularly a trademark of the calisthenics body. Because we don't look to isolate the arms, we have a big chance of liberating the genetic potential of our lats by performing pull-ups, muscle-ups, bar levers, and the human flag. The lats play an egregious role in these kinds of exercise and many others. As you read before about "the human flag" involves a substantial part of abs, lats shoulders and arm strength as well as many other muscles.

Their development is a clear result of a plenty bodyweight pulling program. The shoulders are utilized in all upper body calisthenics strength exercises and get a specific workout from every exercise quoted thus far. When we train handstand push-ups, the "V" formed by the lats gets larger. Even those who think they can military press massive poundage are mostly humiliated when they tray this exercise, but if they keep doing it, they'll eventually discover that handstand push-ups conduct to astronomical gains in the shoulders.

Undoubtedly, the push-up is the greatest of all chest exercises. It can be progressed to bring forth a far more significant punch than the classic version we all know and which is an excellent exercise in its own right. Moreover, we can perform activities like theses while being inclined, while limiting the points of contact or by increasing the range of movement. All of these methods use progressive strategy to build a muscular, hard, powerful chest. That chest will be your lever once you perform the one-arm push-up, which mixes balance, stability, increased the range of motion, and muscular overload in only one exercise.

Calisthenics Arms

Just as with abs, when it comes to arms your best friend is bar work, particularly biceps, which get a better training from chin-ups than from all the curls in the world. The gains are astronomical, and the choices are infinite when you're pulling far more weight than you would typically curl. Do them all overhand pull-ups and underhand chins, thick bar, wide grip and narrow, switch grip and hanging from irregularly shaped objects, and you'll create amazing flexible strength and strong connective tissue. To get forearms that would make Popeye jealous, mix advanced push-up different changes with the grip training you get from bar work. It can demand many machine-based isolation-style exercises to hit the arms, chest, and shoulders from as many angles as the great old-fashioned dips. Well-done deep (going slight lower than 90-degree angle), with all variations' style, the results are indisputable. Try as many different hand widths as possible to get best results. They can also be performed on a bench or straight bar.

Calisthenics Legs

If you settle for body weight to train your legs, they certainly get strong. And it's not because of external resistance, but rather thanks to manipulating gravity and performing all movement types. Bodyweight squats go all the way to the ground I mean ass to ankles. I'm interested in building power through the full expression of a movement. Try doing 50 bodyweight squats all the way down. If you feel it easy, do it anyway just to make sure. And if it is easy, then add five more with only one leg! Workouts like pistol squats use our inborn sense of balance, which unfortunately many of us have lost track all over the years. To get this movement perfect, you must push, pull, and stabilize using all your leg muscles, in a great mixture of strength and mobility. Another calisthenics basics, Back bridging. It demands further recruitment of hamstrings, glutes and spinal erectors. Real strength and excellent flexibility combined will shape the backside of a calisthenics warrior.

The 10 Directives of Calisthenics Muscle Mass

- DIRECTIVE 1: Embrace reps!

- DIRECTIVE 2: Work Hard!

- DIRECTIVE 3: Use Simple, Compound Exercises!

- DIRECTIVE 4: Reduce Sets!

- DIRECTIVE 5: Concentrate on progress and use a Training dairy!

- DIRECTIVE 6: You rise if you Rest. So feel free to take rest!

- DIRECTIVE 7: keep eating clean the whole Time!

- DIRECTIVE 8: Sleep well!

- DIRECTIVE 9: Train your mind while training your Body!

➢ **DIRECTIVE 10: Get Strong!**

In the end, you'll agree that callisthenic exercises are great to build natural strength – easy or hard. The results of intense, exigent, and robust calisthenics exercise will produce incredible results.

How Can You Do Those Exercises At Home Or In The Street?

No need to use equipment. It is not entirely true, but most of the calisthenics exercises do not demand equipment. If there is something to do some pull-ups on then, you are ready to start. On the other hand, you can take a pull-up bar, a door-frame bar for very few bucks. You can make your station as I did with a pull-up bar and dip station if you are creative. In the long run, doing calisthenics will cost you much less than going to the gym, and you can do it whenever you want in the comfort of your home. There is no need to wait for the machines, travel and so on. Moreover, we must not forget there are playgrounds for exercise for free in many cities. I found them by just taking a walk around and being creative.

The Lean & Mean Calisthenics Diet

In addition, to regular workouts techniques to keep stimulating your muscles to grow, you can also get more muscle size and strength by following a diet. Developing a well-sculpted physique demands more than just training. To truly build the desired body that shows off your strong muscles and all your hard work, you must eat right. The calisthenics diet isn't difficult or complicated, but it still requires the same kind of hard work and mental toughness of doing bodyweight exercises.

Follow the Calisthenics workout diet to get calisthenics body you want. If you're ready to commit to the calisthenics diet and want to increase your workout efforts, oblige yourself to eat right and put an end to junk food. That's a right place to begin. And once you're used to eating healthy, the rest is not difficult. The calisthenics diet isn't anything hard. There's no complicated system to follow, no need to take pills or supplements or to buy expensive pre-packaged food.

Here's the strategy for success with this diet:

➤ **Eat As Natural As Possible**

To be lean and mean by rolling through the drive-thru and ordering a hamburger, soft drink, and bucket of fries. And that ripped, and shredded look isn't the result of chocolate bars, energy drinks, and pastries. If you're serious about following the calisthenics diet, you've got to say goodbye to junk food.

➤ **Eat Produce, Organic when Possible**

We all know that fruits and veggies are good, but let's get more information. Whenever you can, try to eat organic produce. More clearly, these are foods that have been grown on farmlands and pastures without synthetic chemical pesticides, food additives, or antibiotic agents for more than three years. So eat organic produce if possible, particularly when you have to eat the skin/peel of the item. If you don't have enough money to buy organic, eat conventional produce, but be sure to wash and scrub it thoroughly.

➢ Get Your Protein IN

You need protein to repair your damaged muscles after a tough bodyweight workout, and that's exactly what you want from a workout. Your muscles need the essential amino acids found in protein after the workout to grow bigger and stronger. To cut down on costs, eat more plant-based protein and buy high-quality animal meat in bulk. Aiming for about 1 gram of protein for each pound of body weight per day is an excellent goal to attain if you're training and trying to build strong muscle. You can do this by eating foods like egg whites, low-fat dairy products like milk and yogurt, nuts and seeds, lean meats and skinless poultry.

If you are a vegetarian; Lacto-ovo-vegetarians (eat both dairy products and eggs); this is the most common type of vegetarian diet. Lacto-vegetarians eat dairy products but avoid eggs. Vegans: (do not eat dairy products, eggs, or any other products which are derived from animals). It is entirely okay if you replace your "meat-intake" by many kinds of beans and nuts, but you will still need to take fish-oil, omega 3 and amino acids supplements to make sure you are getting everything your body needs and even more to grow.

> **Grains and Dairy**

Are gluten and dairy friends or foes? I can't give you a definitive answer. I eat bread and almond milk regularly and have no problems with them, but I know many others who must steer clear of such foods or other suffer bloating, ache, and deficiency of energy. My suggestion: try cutting gluten-rich grains (food including rye, wheat, and barley,) and dairy out of your diet for 30 days, then verify if you feel better or not. The essential thing is that you can always get all your proteins, carbs, fats, and vitamins from non-gluten, non-dairy sources such as meat, potatoes, and veggies, so taking off grains and dairy from your diet will not hurt your workout or your health.

Vegetables, legumes, nuts, fruits and whole grains are healthy. They provide to your essential body vitamins, nutrients, and antioxidants needed to repair cell damage and build strong muscle after a long hard workout. Compared to the kind of food you'll find at a typical fast food joint, those foods are also low in calories, cholesterol, and fat. To commit to a diet based on whole foods will help you lose body fat, and that's what you need to show off your strong muscles and your hard work.

- **Keep a Food Diary:**

    Having a food diary can help you attain those goals. Get a notebook and record all that you eat. You can do this even before you decide to follow the calisthenics diet. It's an excellent way to see what you're eating, count your calories, and look at what doing right and what you need to change.

Chapter 6 - Mistakes To Avoid In Your Diet

Diet is usually an overlooked element of good health. If you put garbage in your body such as processed food and tons of sugar, it will affect your health severely. You will gain weight, and there will be possibilities of developing a multitude of health problems like diabetes and heart disease. Meanwhile, if you provide good stuff to your body, you will get excellent results on the outside. You can't keep eating unhealthy foods just because you are working out. Of course, you are better off than if you just ate that same diet and didn't exercise. But you need to both train and maintain a healthy diet if you want to see real change in your health and body. Most fitness practitioners agree that working out is only 50% of the battle the other 50% is your diet; that is how important it is.

There are two main mistakes that people make in terms of their diet when exercising:

> Mistake 1: Eating unhealthy, processed food.

This includes fast food, ice cream, candy and frozen dinners. You can quickly know if it's a processed food! It often comes in a box doesn't look like a natural food. Nowadays, most of us can realize whether what we are eating is healthy or not; so you just need to refuse. So, follow a healthy, balanced diet including seafood, meat, vegetables, fruits, nuts, and oils.

> Mistake 2: Not getting enough protein.

Protein is the essential building block of muscle. To be clear, I'm not telling you to buy protein shakes and eat protein bars. What I mean exactly is that if you want to get strong muscle through working out, then your diets have to provide you enough protein. So you only have to incorporate a little more into your everyday diet. Food like eggs, chicken, fish and all meats should be a principal part of your daily food if you are looking to build muscle and get power with calisthenics.

You can get lean and mean following the calisthenic diet. It's not that hard. You've got to make up your mind to consume a clean eating plan, and the results will follow. Eat fresh, eat natural, eat whole, and you'll see stunning results in your fitness and health.

Your body is the only piece of equipment you'll ever need to say goodbye to weights. Callisthenics exercises are an accessible form of exercise with a variety of simple motions requiring only your body weight for strength. Lack of equipment is not a pretence for not training. Anyone, at any fitness level, can carry on with what is freely available at any time:

- Your body

- The ground

You will find calisthenic exercises beneficial because it's easy to apply it every day. With calisthenic exercise, you gradually learn to have complete control over your own body. You'll be amazed at what the human body can, or precisely what YOUR body is capable of doing.

Chapter 7 - 30-Day Calisthenics Challenge

Now that you got some basic knowledge of how calisthenics can benefit you and have a better understanding of how it works. Here's our 30-day calisthenics challenge. This fitness challenge will be difficult at first and depending on your current level of fitness you may have to adjust the number of sets and reps to fit your current performance. Each day you will have a series of exercises to perform, and It's highly suggested to keep increasing the number of reps as you begin to feel stronger and stronger.

Before beginning this challenge, I highly recommend you start with a proper warm-up such as:

Warm Up Routine:

1. 2-3 minutes of jump rope (who cares if you mess up, push yourself!)

2. 50 jumping jacks (pull your shoulder blades back, extend arms and focus on the movement)

3. 10 hip extensions

4. 5 hip rotations each leg (like you're stepping over a fence)

5. 10 forward leg swings (each leg)

6. 10 side leg swings (each leg)

7. 10-20 push-ups (scale based on your level of fitness)

8. 10 spiderman steps (each leg)

This may seem like a lot just to warm up, and it may also appear there is a lot to warm up for your hips, butt, legs, and core. These tend to be the muscles that are the tightest and are often overlooked. However, theses muscles are tightest and least active and thus most susceptible to an injury.

The Challenge

Squats

3 sets of 10 reps (10-second rest in between each set)

Reverse Lunge

3 sets of 10 reps (10-second rest in between each set)

Shoulder Press

3 sets of 10 reps (10-second rest in between each set)

Push Ups

3 sets of 10 reps (30-second rest in between each set)

Diamond Press Up

3 sets of 10 reps (30-second rest in between each set)

Reverse Crunch

3 sets of 10 reps (30-second rest in between each set)

Burpees

3 sets of 10 reps (30-second rest in between each set)

Now every week for the next 4 weeks you are to increase the amount of reps by 5. So, week #1 you would be doing 3 sets of 10 reps. Week #2, 3 sets of 15 reps. Week #3, 3 sets of 20 reps and lastly Week #4, 3 sets of 25 reps.

Final Words

Thank you again for purchasing this book!

I really hope this book is able to help you.

The next step is for you to join our email newsletter to receive updates on any upcoming new book releases or promotions. You can sign-up for free, and as a bonus, you will receive a free gift. Our "*Health & Fitness Mistakes You Don't Know You're Making*" book! This book has been written to demystify, expose the top do's and don'ts and to finally equip you with the information you need to get in the best shape of your life. Due to the overwhelming amount of mis-information and lies told by magazines and self-proclaimed "gurus", it's becoming harder and harder to get reliable information to get in shape. As opposed to having to go through dozens of biased, unreliable and un-trustworthy sources to get your health & fitness information. Everything you need to help you has been broken down in this book for you to easily follow and to immediately get results to achieve your desired fitness goals in the shortest amount of time.

Once again, to join our free email newsletter and to receive a free copy of this valuable book, please visit the link and signup now:

www.hmwpublishing.com/gift

Finally, if you enjoyed this book, then I would like to ask you for a favor, would you be kind enough to leave a review for this book? It would be greatly appreciated!

Thank you and good luck in your journey!

About The Co-Author

My name is George Kaplo; I'm a certified personal trainer from Montreal, Canada. I'll start off by saying I'm not the biggest guy you will ever meet and this has never really been my goal. In fact, I started working out to overcome my biggest insecurity when I was younger, which was my self-confidence. This was due to my height measuring only 5 foot 5 inches (168cm), it pushed me down to attempt anything I ever wanted to achieve in life. You may be going through some challenges right now, or you may simply want to get fit, and I can certainly relate.

For me personally, I was always kind of interested in the health & fitness world and wanted to gain some muscle due to the numerous bullying in my teenage years about my height and my overweight body. I figured I couldn't do anything about my height, but I sure can do something about how my body looked like. This was the beginning of my transformation journey. I had no idea where to start, but I just got started. I felt worried and afraid at times that other people would make fun of me for doing the exercises the wrong way. I always wished I had a friend that was next to me who was knowledgeable enough to help me get started and "show me the ropes."

After a lot of work, studying and countless trial and errors. Some people began to notice how I was getting more fit and how I was starting to form a keen interest in the topic. This led many friends and new faces to come to me and ask me for fitness advice. At first, it seemed odd when people asked me to help them get in shape. But what kept me going is when they started to see changes in their own body and told me it's the first time that they saw real results!

From there, more people kept coming to me, and it made me realize after so much reading and studying in this field that it did help me but it also allowed me to help others. I'm now a fully certified personal trainer and have trained numerous clients to date who have achieved amazing results.

Today, my brother Alex Kaplo (also a Certified Personal Trainer) and I own & operate this publishing venture, where we bring passionate and expert authors to write about health and fitness topics. We also run an online fitness website "HelpMeWorkout.com" and I would love to connect with by inviting you to visit the website on the following page and signing up to our e-mail newsletter (you will even get a free book). Last but not least, if you are in the position I was once in and you want some guidance, don't hesitate and ask... I'll be there to help you out!

Your friend and coach,

George Kaplo

Certified Personal Trainer

Download another book for Free

I want to thank you for purchasing this book and offer you another book (just as long and valuable as this book), "Health & Fitness Mistakes You Don't Know You're Making", completely free.

Visit the link below to signup and receive it:

www.hmwpublishing.com/gift

In this book, I will break down the most common health & fitness mistakes, you are probably committing right now, and I will reveal how you can easily get in the best shape of your life!

In addition to this valuable gift, you will also have an opportunity to get our new books for free, enter giveaways, and receive other valuable emails from me. Again, visit the link to sign up:

www.hmwpublishing.com/gift

Copyright 2017 by HMW Publishing - All Rights Reserved.

This document by HMW Publishing owned by the A&G Direct Inc company, is geared towards providing exact and reliable information in regards to the topic and issue covered. The publication is sold with the idea that the publisher is not required to render accounting, officially permitted, or otherwise, qualified services. If advice is necessary, legal or professional, a practiced individual in the profession should be ordered.

From a Declaration of Principles which was accepted and approved equally by a Committee of the American Bar Association and a Committee of Publishers and Associations.

In no way is it legal to reproduce, duplicate, or transmit any part of this document in either electronic means or in printed format. Recording of this publication is strictly prohibited, and any storage of this document is not allowed unless with written permission from the publisher. All rights reserved.

The information provided herein is stated to be truthful and consistent, in that any liability, in terms of inattention or otherwise, by any usage or abuse of any policies, processes, or directions contained within is the solitary and utter responsibility of the recipient reader. Under no circumstances will any legal responsibility or blame be held against the publisher for any reparation, damages, or monetary loss due to the information herein, either directly or indirectly.

The information herein is offered for informational purposes solely, and is universal as so. The presentation of the information is without contract or any type of guarantee assurance.

The trademarks that are used are without any consent, and the publication of the trademark is without permission or backing by the trademark owner. All trademarks and brands within this book are for clarifying purposes only and are the owned by the owners themselves, not affiliated with this document.

For more great books visit:

HMWPublishing.com

www.ingramcontent.com/pod-product-compliance
Lightning Source LLC
Chambersburg PA
CBHW062152100526
44589CB00014B/1805